Better Version of Me

Written By: GES.Tulagan

Combined With Other Side of Me

While every precaution has been taken in the preparation of this book, the publisher assumes no responsibility for errors or omissions, or for damages resulting from the use of the information contained herein.

THE BETTER VERSION OF ME

First edition. May 4, 2024.

Copyright © 2024 GES.TULAGAN.

ISBN: 979-8224590773

Written by GES.TULAGAN.

Table of Contents

I would like to dedicate this book to God for helping me all throough out my journey. For my daughters who inspired me and to my family who supported me. And to all the people that has been part of my life thank you for the experience .

Time

In this world that is full of surprises, Time plays a significant factors for everything. In reality, there are lots of the things that can define time, depending on the situation, events and people and places. But one thing is for sure that time is one of a few things that money cannot buy. And we are given a free will on how we can use and manage it properly.

Somehow, when you felt sad, lost and without any direction, that makes you feels time is so slowly moving that make you scared, stressed and depressed. And you might wish that you have the ability to know when your time on earth will end. But in reality we really do not have that ability, so instead dwell on the positive side and reflect on how you can make the most of your time during this trial, and make the most of it while we are still given the chance to live and survive in this cruel world.

We all know from the beginning that life is really unfair, we may never get what we want and the information that we need to know to become successful. But this also give us the ability to improve learned from the mistake, and become a better version of ourselves. We can choose to be positive and optimistic to get a positive results out of a negative situation that we have at the moment. Time really heals all wounds and pains, and the scars that are left is reminder that you survived all those unfortunate experience through God's grace.

All these challenges in life, it will either make a person bitter or better. The experience that we learned from our time can either make us a good or bad person. Sometimes we are not aware on what we become, because all we know is how to survive and try to live at that time. One thing is for sure that people can change in an instant either for best or for worst depending on how the person react on this challenging time.

Always remember no one can judge you for what you become but you have an option to choose to become a better version of yourself based on the negative experience at that time. You can still correct the mistake that you made and restart your life through God' grace. Always ask for God's guidance because at the end of our life only God can judge us. We might fail over and over again as good Christian, but as long as you keep your faith and your communication with God you will see that time of challenges and trials are made to be there for you to become stronger, bolder on your decision in life. So even on the negative situation you can use your time wisely and reflect on your purpose, while waiting for the end of your time on Earth, since nothing is permanent in this World.

LOVE

As per Bible verse definition of love is kind, patience, it's not boastful, is not proud of doing wrong things. Love is a four letter word, a powerful word that everyone can experience and feel even though we can't see it on our naked eye. However through a person's action we are able to view and feel what love is. Powerful enough to make you better or a disaster, love can also break you or fix you. It is a kind of feeling that you are willing to sacrifice in exchange of it. Sacrifice your happiness for your loved ones because you truly love them.

Even you will walk through the shadow of valley of death, you will not be shaken because you know that God loves you and he gave his only son for you to be save. God sacrifices His son for our sins and love us unconditionally, so we need to learn how to love the same. Though we are only human and commit a lot of mistake and wrong choices, God's love is so powerful that He give us a lot of chances and strength to move on as if nothing happen. That is how His love work in my life. I commit a lot of sin, a lot of mistake and a lot of wrong decision but His always there to listen at the lowest time of my life.

In this generation and in this imperfect world we might be ended disappointed about love that we are expecting, because only God can give us the unconditional love that we are searching and looking for. There is no perfect love that we can offer because we are human and we are not perfect. But if we will see how God loves us then we can also love our family, friends neighbour and enemy with our human imperfect way. We can be transform from being the black sheep of the family to become the apple of the eye of God. Because once we accept the love of Jesus for us we became his children.

As long as you are not hurting other physically, emotionally, verbally, and spiritually intentionally or unintentionally, I thought that is enough to be a good person. But thanks to all the experience abroad and right now that I lost my job and unemployed. It made me realize how my family love me without nothing to give in return. In spite of not helping them during their problems because I am also drowning on my own problem before. You can see that even I am not being good with them they still love me and help me though it all. And I know that God allow it to happen to change my perspective in life. I might hurt other people emotionally and physically intentionally or unintentionally and I am not proud of it. But that is how God test my patience and ability. God is checking your personality if you will remain in calmness and peace in midst of trials. God is teaching me how to love without expecting something in return. To see that sometimes being kind is better than being right. God uses other people to change your perception in life.

In this journey called life that train me how to survive on all the challenges of life. With the help of God's love I was able to continue and make it through. With my existence I learned how God's love is so amazing that he usually remove those things that we thought that are important for us to see and reflect on our life. I may not know my purpose of existence in this world but I know with God's love I am able to conquer all the challenges that I will face because He is with me.

The beauty of God's love is it gives us contentment, contentment for what we have and appreciate what we currently have right now. It is also teach us to be humble because you will be needing help from other people and now I learned that it is no one is an island. Because before, I am overly focus on myself that become greedy for the things that I want to experience and unable to help because I have my own goal and target. But God did not allow it to be successful, because He is teaching me how to love and to correct the wrong doing that I consistently had done.

Amazing right how you can see all the mistake that you made and He still love you the same way. And that is how God's Love work. So if you are currently experiencing challenges and trial you can try to reflect on what God is trying to teach you and always remember that God Love is enough to save you and He will be with you at all time. Just listen to His Word and there will be a voice and instinct that will guide you along the way. I am grateful for His love because I found peace and calmness. Of course I am only human I still make a lot of mistake and wrong decision but I am thankful for God's love and mercy that help me to wake up with greatness on day to day living.

WE SHOULD BE THANKFUL for every day, because we are given another chance to live in this world and it will be a new experience and another experience that we will gain

LIFE

Life is a precious gift from our Father up above. It's a journey given to you by God and that start when you were born. Life is full of choices, to do what is right or what is wrong. Life is also a game, we can win in living or lose by dying. Life is unfair that is what they say and what I had experience but even if it is unfair I believe that life is a choice. Before I wonder why people are committing suicide, murder and abortion. And when I aged as a person I see the reason why they try to commit it. This world is like a battle field people are struggling to live because of lacked of money, food, water, clothing, job, and most of all people lacked the communication and faith in God. There are no longer hope within themselves to continue in this so called life. That is sad truth about life but the good news is God will never allow thing to happen without any reason and perhaps it will uncover the hidden lesson that you need to learn about life.

In life we need to be strong, strong enough physically, mentally emotionally and spiritually to survive on a daily basis with God's grace. As a human I learned that inner peace and contentment is one of the key to peaceful life. And the world will try to distract you, provoke you to be on war on a daily basis. But the good thing is when you have an inner peace and calmness and God's guidance nothing could take that away from you. What is meant to be yours will always find its way back to you. Of course we are all human sometimes we will failed but failure is just a beginning of another attempt to be a successful person someday.

As they say when life throw you a bunch of lemon then create a lemonade. And when one door of a job opportunity closes that is not the end of the world but beginning of a new job hunting. When you do not have a job that is the beginning to look for your passion and plan what you want in life. Just listen to your instinct because it is like a guide that helps you make a right decision. If only I trust it from the start perhaps I committed less mistake. But I don't regret it because I learned from all the mistake that I committed and God is always there to help me when I needed Him. He always uses people around me to help me. Before when I am blind of it I always think that I am tired of helping others because I am burned up with my day to day living until God remove everything that physically and personally matter to me and made me realize the importance of helping people in need. That we are all living with His grace and mercy.

As long as you are breathing God is giving you a chance to look for your purpose, purpose that until now I cannot find, and that hunting of purpose is the reason why I am still living see it is like a cycle. Like on a company that people were hired at the beginning and resigned when living. It like having a life when we were born and it will end when we die.

People say we need to live our life to the fullest because we only live once. Yes but I want to live my life fulfilling my responsibility as a mother and to see my daughters success and happiness in life. Simple thing it might seem but the struggle is real. But hoping one day I can see it if God's will and He will still give me time to experience that. Only God knows our future and know when it will end. So right hoping to live on a daily basis trying not to worry what the future might be and trust God on His perfect timing. To live and to search for our purpose.

Choose to be happy, because happiness is a choice.

HAPPINESS

Happiness is a state of emotion of a person having an extra joy and satisfaction. Being happy will not cost you any penny. And it is a choice you can take in spite of or despite of hard times, trial and challenges. Call it crazy but it is a great help for you to make it through the storm of problems. Remember even if you will be sad, lonely and losing hope to resolve the problem that set of emotion will not fixed the problem that you are going through. But these set of emotion will only dragged you to a depression. It is not bad to be sad or lonely, but you can also choose to be happy during the trial times.

When you feel that the world is falling apart, it is hard to remain and maintain your inner peace your calmness and happiness. But one thing that I can guarantee you is once you learn to control your emotion, your inner peace and you can choose what is best for you nothing will go against your life. It might be hard as it will be but letting go of everything we can't control will give as happiness and inner peace. It is easy being said specially if you think that I did not experience it, but believe me or not it really work for me. Like a lesson learned form a video in Facebook if you will be holding the glass of water for a couple of minute you can bare it but if you will be holding the glass of water for 12 hours straight, you will not endure it and become numb till you let go of the glass that your holding because you cannot bare it anymore. Same way with our problem if we will keep on thinking of the problem, it will not be resolve but we will end up frustrated about it. But if we chose to let go and let God do the rest, then nothing can be wrong. As for me if there are lots of problem arise during application and it give me instinct not to do it. Even as much as I need the job I will let it go because almost all my instinct are correct. And that is when I decided to be happy at times of trial and problem. I do not want to waste my time on regretting the mistake that I made but I want to use my energy on the things that I am still able to do and choose to be happy.

Though this state of emotion is temporary because nothing is permanent except changes, it will still give you the stamina to move forward to restart and make a new plan for you future. Life is a roller coaster journey, sometimes you are up doing great and sometimes you are down at your lowest point of your life. For all the people who are experiencing hell on our journey called life the best advice that I can provide is to choose to be optimistic, to choose yourself and to choose what will make your life happy and let go of the pain, hurt and problem. Let it resolve itself and you will heal and can start a new plan. And one day you will be amaze on the results and thank God for those problem you been through.

CHOOSE THE ROAD THAT will bring you to your goals, dreams and happiness.

CHOICE

Everyday God gave us free will to choose what we want to accomplish in life. From the moment that we wake up we have an option to wake up or continue to go back to sleep. If you choose to wake up, you need to decide again if you will choose to start your household chores or fix yourself first, and so on and so forth. You see we all have a choice, we can be good or bad depending on our current situation. Whatever our decision and path in life that we follow our belief and aspiration, hoping that we will choose our self, because that it is something worth fighting for. And always remember that for every mistake that we commit there is always a way to make it better. You just need to choose your happiness. It is easy than being done that is what they say but if it is the only thing that you are holding on I can guarantee you that it is worth it. Its peaceful living on daily routine letting go of those things that stressed us the most. And that is one of the perfect choice that you can make for yourself.

There is consequence of the free will that God gave us, because there is always am effect for the action that we choose. But we can always charge it to experience and compile the lesson learned for that specific situation. And be wise in case we encounter it again. It is sad to say that sometimes or often times we cannot choose what is right because there are things that we need to sacrifice for the said decision. Since we are only human we always commit wrong decision but if we are already on the said situation, just always be calm, relax and gather yourself again together to start an new plan to choose to restart. Time flies too fast we will not notice that we already aged and overcome a lot of problem and trials in life. And the big question is have we ever choose ourselves? That is the biggest question I would like to leave with you.

As for me I just learned it recently to choose myself even though I am wrong because at the end of the day if you will be affected and your inner peace will be shaken it is not worth the damage it will cause you. It might destroy the self-healing that I hardly learned. Yes I am wrong yes I am sinful and yes I made a lot of wrong choice. But this time I will chose myself and to die for myself and that is what I choose right now. And this wrong decision that I made is also an effect of what they have done to me so I called it quits and peace for all. So starting right now I will choose myself and choose to be happy on what I have. If things will not go my way then let it be let me be stuck to my own world with my inner peace and calmness. Be bold on what I think is right and surpasses all the trial in life it might not be to the excellent record, but least I tried to choose myself and be myself and accept my good and bad side if the story.

Move on, your mistake is just a proof that you are a human being. Move on and conquer the world.

REGRET

Regret is a product of a wrong choice in life that we made, it will always at the end or it is a results of decision that we made that is unsuccessful. Of course, if you will know the end result at the beginning you will not take the risk of that decision. Or will you still do it because you like taking risk and see if it will make a positive results in spite of knowing the risk then you are 100 percent risk taker. Or if the person does not have a courage to take it they might missed the opportunity because of they are coward to take the risk. See you might be confused where you can stand your perspective in life to be coward to commit a risk or a risk taker that will gamble everything to check if they are right?

As for me since I committed a lot of mistake and wrong choices and decision. I have regret it but I tried to divert it to another life lesson learned. I need to overcome it so that I can move on and restart. Otherwise you will end up frustrated depressed and nothing to hold on to. Remember our mistake will not make us a less of a person but a mistake is a proof that we are only human that can make a wrong choice. Sometimes I felt that I am a failure because of the wrong decision that I made, but every time felt it I can feel the presence of God saying I made it happen for your own good. I know that God doesn't want bad choices or hobby or doing, but it is one way of telling you Hey it is not yet the end of the world to restart and refocus.

Life is too short to be wasted by our regret. On all the mistake that we commit in the past. So even though this world is difficult to live in be strong and brave enough to take the results of the wrong decision that you made. Add it to the life lesson learned and make it a stepping stone to become a better version of yourself. I never said always make a wrong decision and do not regret it but what I am saying is all things that happens is for a reason. Always remember that you have a family to be taken care of that love you and accept you for who you are. If you do not have a family we have our God who is always there to listen and walk with us through our journey in Earth. We need to move on from regret and accept what the future will be. These may be difficult to apply but eventually you will laugh at it when you overcome it.

Do not pretend, just be yourself and show your positive and negative side and see who will stay.

ATTITUDE

Attitude is define as a character of a person. They said it is more powerful than hardworking and intelligent. Because you may know everything and can work hard for it but if you do not have a good attitude everything will not fall into places. But is it really attitude that will define a person? What if the reason of her character is a results on how the world made her /him on what her/his belief, on what she experience and how she see the meaning of life. Do you have the right to judge her/him for the decision and choices and attitude that they gain?

Some also say their attitude is depending on how the other person treat them, is that right? Do we need to do the same? These are simple question but come to think of it does that made the person attitude right. As for me I am not perfect but if you already created a wall between yourself and other person you will no longer be affected on their attitude. Because that is a reflection of their character not yours and just tried to understand that they may be going through a difficult situation. Of course I am also human and there are limit of thing that I can tolerate but if I cannot take it anymore it is better to walk out and protect your inner peace.

We may have a different attitude, because we had a different experience and circumstances in life. And whatever the attitude, manner and character of that person is showing you, hoping that we are not quick to judge them because everyone is only human that person might have a trauma and had a bad experience in life that made them who they are today. They said we are all on the same storm but some are riding a boat and some are riding a yacht during that same storm so do not compare how you survive the storm because you did know the whole story. Yes our past experience is what made us who we are today and we are also responsible for our choices. So what I can do in this situation is smile back, walk away, or if you can try to joke around and let them realize their mistake. And it will create a peaceful life for you and for the other person.

In this society that sets what is right and wrong, what is important and what is not, what is normal and what is abnormal, then tell me what is the right attitude that we need to have to be included in this society which personality should we mimic to be included. As for me I will not change my self just to be included, if my attitude will not fit in to your standard then make an equal standard for all the people. I won't change myself just to be loved and to belong, we are all created unique so I think acceptance is the more important than attitude.

COMMITMENT

It is a 10 letter word that make you believe in forever. But the reality it is like a promise that tend to be broken. Sounds bitter but it makes your mind stronger than your heart to make any decision making about it. Commitment is a fulfilment of a promise it can be to others to work or to yourself. You need to do everything you can to fulfil it. Sometimes due to several circumstances that might come along the way, like a temptation that is a major cause of sin, we tend to fall for it and forget about our commitment that we abide to. In the end what is important is that we tried our best to accomplish and fulfil the commitment that we give, whether we failed or not at least we learned.

Trust is a fundamental factor of a relationship and once trust are broken it is hard to repair the relationship same goes with commitment. That is the reason I no longer believe in marriage, because it is like a contract paper issued to give you the legality of partnership, what if two people are no longer happy with each other and even if they will try their best to be together it seems like it is not working. Will they be living for the sake of the contract that they signed? Yes we can forgive but it doesn't mean that it will be the same as before. Like a vase that was broken and you tried to fixed it, you can make it a whole vase but a little damage will break that vase again. Yes we forgive for our inner peace but doesn't mean that they are welcome to come back.

My defend mechanism is not to expect and believe in forever, because life is not a fairy tales that you can get a happy ending. You can commit to love but always make a habit of loving yourself more. That is not being selfish but you need to protect yourself to be broken and to be damage because it is so hard to fixed yourself it will take time for you to heal and that will be the time that you will no longer believe in commitment. Or you can still forgive and chances are history will just repeat itself so be ready to be broken again. And the decision is always yours to make.

By committing to care for myself, I made a mistake to sacrifice the job that I had for a peace of mind. There are few regret but overall I am happy to let it go I may be broke but I am happy stress free and most of all I still have my inner peace and calmness. If I choose to stay perhaps I come back to all my vices because of stressed. I may not have money as of the moment but I believe another door will open that will help me to continue what I started with, and not to temp me go back to my vices. I am thankful for that incident because at least I was able to retain what I started it may be the wrong way but it gives a positive results.

Therefore before you commit or make a commitment, make sure that you are personally, physically, emotionally and spiritually complete. Because eventually it will be tested in time you may fail or succeed but the good thing is you will learned a lot from that experience. And make sure not to lose yourself during the process, and if it will affect you mentally and physically let it go self-care self-love and your devotion to it is more important than anything else. It is very hard to recover once you lose yourself, it will take a lot of time preparation and mind set for you to move on and some people is unable to recover from hurt and pain.

DESIRE

Have you ever felt feeling wanted and needed by other person? Have you ever felt self-satisfaction? Have you ever felt that the world is so amazing to live that makes your heart beats faster? Have you ever felt the inner peace that make your soul at ease? Have you ever been frustrated and become contented at the end? Have you ever lost but eventually realize your worth? Did you imagine yourself being the person that you desire to be when you were young? Have you ever felt you change a lot for better and even for worst but still felt so secure and at peace. Have you ever?

I can say a reason for all the question ask has a reason. We might not understand it in our own perception but eventually we will learn our purpose. Sometimes our desire to become better and to fit in to the society that put a standard what is right and wrong and what is moral and immoral who are acceptable and who are not. But come to think of it we are not here to change ourselves just to fit in. We have a different personality. All I can say is that we need to know and accept ourselves for who we are and not for other perspective of who we are, then you will see the clarity. Once you let go of other people opinion, then you will be able to see and know your true desire. Sometimes you will be surprised because once they can no longer control you, you will be able to see how more peaceful your surroundings will be. I may not have and achieve what I desire when I was a little kid, but I am happy and at peace with myself right now.

BEING CRAZY, NAUGHTY and a joker sometimes makes life a little lighter you just need to balance it.

CRAZY MADNESS

When you no longer care about the world. You already reach your maximum potential. Because the world can no longer control you. This point might be too dangerous while giving you an inner peace at the same time. The desire to be part of this world is no longer your goal. And yet you still have the power to make things possible.

Sometimes you do not need to control everything, because accept it or not some situation are out of our control. This is consider a test of your personality and patience while waiting for a sunshine after the rain. You already pass different storm to be bother by another storm of life. This will gauge how we will react and deal with another trial. I am not proud of the mistake that lead to a hell of an experience, but I am positive that life in hell will end eventually. Stay with me right now or not thru my hell journey, I will still wake up and find my way out.

You can no longer affect my state of emotion, with your harsh words, works and action. Because I already build a wall that will guard me against your evil attempt to break me. Your words is just a waste because I know myself better today, my good side , my bad side, my beautiful version and ugliest version that you can imagine. Yes all of it I accept and love who I am right now. Call me crazy but I am just being true to myself.

Sometimes is heaven sometimes is hell, here I am still breathing, ready to face the battle of life on a daily basis. Some battle I win some I lose, but it doesn't matter at all, what matter most is the experience that I gain and the lesson that I learned. Having my own space and walls is easy because you thought me how to defend my peace that way. So do not dare me to change with the old version of myself because I will not I so love the new version of me now. The peaceful, the calmer the crazy person that I become right now.

I may not have all the desire, wishes longings that I want before as of the moment. It will not stop my imagination to reach all the things that I want and deserve. It may not be real but God knows the next thing that might happen and I might have all of it. Just relax and try to enjoy the moment while waiting patiently for the next move that we will take.

WHATEVER YOU WILL DO people tend to say you positive and negative about your action. You are not born to make them happy. Just be real and true to yourself.

REAL ME

I was lost in this world, and didn't know how to restart for a while. I felt so alone and looking for my mission. Until one day I realize, being alone is not bad and it will make you realize your worth. It will also show you the other world.

Thank you! For making me realize my worth. Thank you for making me feel the world. And for me feeling alone against all odds of the world. I may be right I may be wrong but it doesn't matter anymore. As long as I am contented, mentally stable I will stay calm and peaceful with all the challenges of life. My past will not define me as a person and I will not be bother what other's opinion about me. In the first place I need to thank them for all the treatment and experience that I encounter, it made me realize that they are not important in my decision making.

I may be the worst person that you can think of, liar, sinner, crazy, and doesn't have the right manner to the standard that this world set for living. I will not be bother because you doesn't have the right to judge me as a person because you are not God. Only God can judge me for what I become right now. Whatever you will say, it will no longer affect me because this world train me to become numb. Numb enough to build a wall for other person that tries to harm and take the little sanity and calmness in my own world.

In life it is not always in your favour, sometime you will feel sad, happy, loved, loneliness and accepted. It is like on a snap of a finger where your emotion can change depending on what will trigger you. But the good news is you can control how you will respond, you can decide and choose what you want. As long as you have the courage to take the risk and face the consequence it will bring.

Every time I looked at the mirror, I can see my reflection. And guess what that person aged and not be beautiful in your perspective, not morally righteous. But what I see is a survivor, a brave soul that is always trying to survive in this cruel world. I no longer care about your negative feedback about me, I will just get what is best for me other opinion is like a waste that I need to throw in the trash can where it belong. I will no longer change just to make everyone happy because I deserve to be happy and be myself in my own way.

So I stand up for myself, and I will do what will make me happy. And I will not wait for someone else to make myself feel better so that I will not end up disappointed.

To My Mom

Lately you always visit me in my dream, in my dreams it seems you are real alive and truly conversing with me. Thank you because you still care even if you are not physically here on Earth. Please do not worry about me, ever since I was a child I already encounter how to survive in this world. At young age you already trained me how to survive and I thank you for making me an independent strong person that I am today. I am not proud on all my past mistake this might be intentional or unintentional, but that make me the person I am today.

I know that before you left you knew that I am also a mother. I tried my best to provide for hem and perform my duties as a mother and love them unconditionally. I know I had a lot of secret that I kept from you and I may not be your perfect daughter that you wanted. Now I know how hard it is to be a mother and now I know how you felt. This is really a one of a kind experience that you can imagine, it seems easy but it is really hard. Please do not worry about a closed doors that are not meant for me, eventually I believe that there will be a great opportunity waiting on the right time. And I am thankful right now for all the people who is helping me at the moment on my current situation.

Being a mother is very a broad responsibility. In this unfair world where as a father just have a job and can provide for their children are already considered good father. But a mother who is also working and doing household chores is sometimes not enough to be a good one. Yes I know that life is really unfair and accept that reality but sometimes it is really unfair.

I know that you are worried lately that is the reason you always visit me in my dreams. I also remember how we argue about life and you mention that I will miss you when you were gone and yes you are correct about it. I just want to let you know that I will be fine and this strong girl that you raised will make it till my last breath on earth. Like what I said you raised a survivor, with God's grace everything will be alright. Thank you for everything and till we meet again.

The Better Version of Me

Written By: GES.Tulagan

REJECTION

What is your point of view about rejection? Would you take it on a positive or negative perception? Have you ever felt being rejected? How many times did you encounter it? These are few question that will leave a mark and you will wonder why rejection happen. And you might be wondering who would like the feeling of being rejected, and of course the answer is no one.

Whatever your take about rejection, whether you will take it on a positive or negative side, please remember that rejection will not gage your personality, or your character as a human being. As I listen to father Fidel while he conduct his mass, He define rejection as a protection. Perhaps God is leading you to a different path and God is protecting you from evil doing that will create self-destruction. And that is the reason why God did not allow things to happen to redirect you to the correct path, which is absolutely correct. There are many thing that we are unable to control in life. But one thing that we can control is how to response to it. If we will be optimistic it might create a positive result. Because you will not stress yourself out thinking of the question why did it happen? You might be disappointed but you will not blame yourself with that because you will be thinking that there might be a greater opportunity that will be meant for you. Unlike if you will take it on the negative side that might create anger, hatred and self-destruction and you might be stock with negative emotion and unable to move on. That is why I am encouraging everyone to be optimistic about negative situation such as rejection. Because one of the beauty of learning to control your emotions and response s is that you will felt that you are at peace not only to yourself but also to others.

As a conclusion, in the world whereas stress is constantly affecting each individual on a daily basis, we need to take control take charge to our respond and emotion. It might be hard at the beginning but I can guarantee you that you will get used to it. The best thing that we can give our self is a peace of mind and letting go of the negative emotion and situation like rejection. And believe me that this will conquer your fear to be left alone, because sometimes being alone is a good opportunity to lead you to self-love and acceptance, and you might realize what you really want to do in life. We need to see the positive side to the negative situation to be strong, to be brave, to be a survivor, and to be a better version of our self because we are born to be a survivor.

Daughters

Babies are God's special gift to a woman. Not everyone is given the opportunity to become a mother of their own flesh and blood. It is an honour to be blessed by a baby, and it is a blessing that comes with greater responsibility. This will give you a fulfilment of another milestone on your motherhood journey. You will carry the baby for nine months inside your body, until the day that the baby will be born and have a glance in the world. It is a magical moment because on the day that the baby is born, they are able to breathe on their own, drink milk with your breast and create a small gesture and action on their tiny body. A miracle it is that life is a cycle that begin when you were born and end when you die.

I am blessed having two pretty daughters, two different personality and beauty that tested my patience and capability. They are the source of my strength, my motivation to work and my sanity. Having a daughters is not an easy job, but gives me an incredible feeling of satisfaction. Beyond my imperfection as a human I am given an opportunity to raised two daughters that I can call my own. I may not be able to control how they speak think and act but I can guide them with their journey in this life. My mistake in the past is something that I want to use for them to not experience and make the same mistake that I made. They let me experience everything I need to know to become a mother. I am not perfect but I tried the best that I can be to be a good mother to them. They also bring the best and worst of my personality, because they will test your patience and love along the way. With this two lovely person I learned, I changed and transform to another human being.

So I believe that everything happen for a reason, and being blessed with two daughter is a lifetime responsibility and you need to be emotionally, spiritually, and physically prepared because it is indeed another roller coaster experience with a purpose. They are one of the reason for a better version of me today.

Family

Family is a group of people that is consisting of a mother, father, brother, sister, grandfather, grandmother, auntie, uncle, cousins, granddaughter and grandsons that are connected thru blood lines. These people are the first human being we have an interaction from the day we are born unless you have a different situation. They have a big role in our life, some can influence you to become a good Christian some can influence you to a negative vices and more. But no matter what it is your life and this is your full responsibility. You will have an option to adopt and you also have an option to be different. Being part of a family is a blessing especially if they can accept you for who you are and what you are capable of doing.

I am grateful with my family. I came from a broken family and at the age of nine I experience a lot of difficulty in life. But I take it as a great experience from my childhood and to my motherhood. With the help of my kind family I overcome lots of problem I encounter thru that journey. All the difficulty in the past are only life lesson learned today. I may not understand it when I was young but right now along the way I do understand the behaviour of other relatives towards me. We may have misunderstanding, anger, hatred sometimes but in times of difficulty I can count on them even I cannot reciprocate it. There are times that I feel alone but that is my choice because I believe that my life is my full responsibility and I need to face the consequences of my action. That is why I am grateful for the extended help they offer during my difficult times and they accept me for who I am and my positive and negative side.

I strongly recommend to value each family member, because you will never know what future will bring. Value and accept each other differences attitude and personality. They are only human and may make a lot of mistake but we are not a judge because only God can judge us. We may be a victim, suspect or witness in life but we do not have a right to judge unless that is a profession that you are into. All we can contribute to our family is to be our self and to become a better version of our self.

Appreciation / Inclusion

It is an extreme feeling once all your effort is being appreciated. It is really a great experience if you felt a sense of being accepted and appreciated, and the feeling of being included as a part of the company or group the feeling of being important person as an employee, or important person to someone's life. Thru your positive and negative qualities, they welcome you and accept your opinion without judging your past. How peaceful it is once you no longer need to pretend just to please other people and make them like you and appreciate you.

In the past, I tried to pretend to be someone else just to be like and love by the people that surrounds me. I exert a lot of effort just to be appreciated and be included. But today, I show my real personality, attitude, and manner, my positive and negative side and see who will remain by my side, who will accept me, who will be remove out of my life. I no longer make extra miles just to be accepted and be included. If it affect my inner peace and I felt that I do not fit in or sense that I no longer belong and if there is already unfair treatment I just leave just to protect myself. And it is indeed a peaceful feeling, the process might be financially tough but it is worth the shot. On the contrary if you are being appreciated, being included and the feeling of being important person as a part of organization or group of people it is an amazing feeling that you are at peace. However since on the perfect world that life is unfair, you often felt that you were left behind, you are not appreciated, and not included and always last to have an access, salary, last to get all the benefits that you are entitled with. I know how difficult it is, but I do not lose my hope that there is a better opportunity or reason behind that. And always remind myself that better days will be coming, a better job offer perhaps or a new adventure awaits. Like I always saying that on a negative situation comes a new redirection. When we were young we tend to do our best just to get what we want and be recognize and appreciated so that we can felt the inclusion. But now I realize that is totally wrong. You need to show your true personality and if you are still appreciated, and included and accepted hose are already add on. That is the reason today I just focus on myself, letting go of negativity and searching for my purpose. I reveal my true colors on my dark days and sunshine. I no longer make an extra effort just to be included, because often times I do not have a control on it. I reveal my true personality and let go of people that is unable to appreciate an accept me just to protect my sanity. One thing that I learned in life is to control your emotion because it is indeed a peaceful feeling.

I strongly recommend to make the best effort for self-improvement, rather than making an effort to be accepted on the community or work. Let of the people that is not helping you to heal and try to have an optimistic perception to get a positive result. Loving yourself is your main responsibility before others, so I am strongly recommending to just be a better version of yourself.

New Beginning

Life is cycle, there is beginning and ending. Life begin when you were given your first heartbeat in your mom's womb and life ended when you die. And there are stages in your life like childhood days, teenager days and college days, working days, and more. And for every stages there is always a beginning to restart a new phase of your life. The good thing is that as long as you are still breathing you are still given a chance to restart renew and reset. It may be a painful process but as long as you're an optimistic along the process with the help of God from up above and your hard work nothing is impossible.

New beginning is not just for people who were given a chance to live after a life death situation, it can be associated to work, or a different situation like a broken relationship. But let me focus on work first, before we often think that work is our life because it is the source of our income. We are often stressed because if it is not working that way as it be. And we tried to do everything just to make or retain our job to fulfil our financial obligation to our family. But is it worth it to be our caused of anxiety, negative attitude and self-destruction? It take me a long time to realize to let go of the job that is destroying my inner peace and sanity. It is a good thing that God allow me take an opportunity to work abroad to experience and learned a lot of lesson in life. I learned to value my freedom that I have in the Philippines. I may not applied it to the first company that I worked with when I come back because of the negative emotions and toxic account process that I encounter, but there is a great lesson that I gain to value my inner peace that process might be incorrect but I can say I successfully protect myself from vices maintain my calmness on a rough days of transition because it financial affect me. Prevention is better than damaging yourself along the process. That is the reason why it gives me a courage to restart, reset and move on. As of the moment it is indeed difficult financially but I am happy about the outcome and how I see things through. I may not have money as of the moment but I am happy that I am able to avoid vices. It seems that history repeat itself but I will not hesitant to do it again. If you felt that it is about to destroy your self care that you are working for years now just let it go and perhaps another doors will open for you that you no longer felt to be left behind. When we make a mistake we still have an option to reset, restart and move on, we can always have a new beginning, new set of goal to improve our way of living, new perception, new attitude and better version of our self. So if you notice that it is bringing the worst out of you think of another option another way to escape that situation.

Letting go and ending this might be a painful process financially and emotionally, but as long as you do it on purpose I believe that it is worth the change you want to happen. Just remember that as long as the purpose is for your sake and for your own peace of mind it will never go wrong. Do not dwell on the pain, the pain is just temporary once you overcome and restart a new work you will be back on your feet and will be financially stable again. Use all the trauma, the negative feeling to become stronger, bolder wiser and to be a better version of yourself. Whatever you might become today is product of all the hardship, trials, challenging that you overcome in the past. So do not stop, you did not come this far just to be left alone but you survive a lot of storm to be bother by a raindrops. And perhaps that there is a special door that is prepared only for you. Just reset, restart, and be open for a new opportunity another doors might open for you to become a better version of yourself.

YOU LEARN

Train your mind to see the beauty of the negative situation so that it will create a positive results.

Mind Set

When you are making a decision are you using your mind or your heart? When you need to choose something do you based it on what you think is right or based on your emotion? When facing a difficult situation do you solve it using a critical and logical thinking or based on what you feel is right?

When you come to the point, where you bleed in love, and wounded your innocent, and your truest were scars and your old habit were buried, or make it short you lived in hell, you tend to use your head or brain compare it to your heart. By using your brain and head in making a decision you are trying to resolve it on a logical and critical thinking and you can be on a positive mind set on a negative situation. Unlike when you use your heart to resolve the situation, you will feel the negative emotion such as madness anger hatred that will cause anxiety and your mind set that will provide greater result. Remember that what you are setting in your mind is powerful, since there is a big chances to make that happen. However if your mind set is negative it will also create negativity. It is like a domino effect what you usually thinking might be your reality. So I strongly recommend to be positive thinking rather than negative thinking. If you felt that your situation is stagnant and there are no longer a growth within, perhaps you need to set a new mind set and be open to a new opportunity and be more productive and think that better days are coming. It happen to us to test how we will react and all we need to show is our real colors that we do not tolerate less than what we deserve. We might be just staying because we do not have a choice but show them that we can still look for a better opportunity that will value as an individual. But of course it requires a lot of hardwork and perseverance to make it happen. Just remember that when you input a plan on your mind you need to take a leap of action to make it happen. Because even if you are a positive person but you are not doing anything to make it happen it will not create any positive results. So always have a positive mind set to become a better version of yourself

People will come and go in your life, just cherish each moment because you will never know what tomorrow will bring.

People

People are individual person that is created by Almighty God. People have their unique personality behaviour. Environment, and also people affect their well-being and their perception in life. People have their own mental capacity, physical capability and emotions on different circumstances of life.

Based on my experience, I learned that people come and go, like changes that is constant in life, people in our life may be available for a quite some time and be gone by the wind with just one snap. It is mainly because we really do not have a control of other's life and their destiny. Some also comes in your life to teach you a lesson and some will be a blessing. As for me when I do a self-evaluation I can say that I have done both a blessing to some and also a worst lesson learned to some. I am not proud on what I did in the past, but there is my personal reason behind that. People may be a cause of your pain and the reason why you no longer trust them. As for me I no longer believe in hearsay, with people I only believe to see is to believe, I only believe in God that even I haven't seen I have faith that his word is true. Because expectation will just disappoint you. Whatever they bring just embrace it and plan ahead on what will be your next action. Perhaps God is trying to redirect you to a new beginning. Once you are able to control your emotion nothing can shake your investment in your peace of mind. For those mistake that I made whether it may be intentionally or unintentionally I apologized for it, perhaps everything happen for a reason. As for me those painful experience that I gain with other people is just part of my past and a lesson learned, it help me a lot to make a boundaries and wall to protect my sanity, my peace of mind. That is the reason that before I will open up with someone I tried to observe first if they will be able to accept my positive and negative side, because I also have a down time, I also experience burn out. And I need to make sure that they are also capable of handling my attitude. Because sometimes as much as I wanted to control my mouth the negative word is automatically coming out. But one thing that I am happy with leaning the boundaries and giving limitation is for myself, to become the better version of myself I might not apply it on all the situation but I am happy with the result of my wall with other people. The sad truth of life is when you are no longer important and if you no longer have anything to offer you will be left behind. That is the reason why there are homeless crazy people because no one is willing to take care of them after they become emotionally damage by people or sometimes it is by a different situation. And the sad part in life is that when gadget and appliances is already malfunctioning others tend to buy it and repair it, but when it comes to people they will just do not care anymore. Hoping that the government can create a project for these people and create a project that they can do to have some things that they can do and still have value in the community. I myself is unable to help because I am not capable of it financially and I do not want to stress myself thinking of a solution, because I need to prioritized as well myself to get back on my feet eventually. I do not want to make it hard for me because I cannot give something that I do not have. So I am just being positive that everything happens for a reason. We may not understand the reason behind but I am just trusting the process and hoping everything will be better in time for every people in the world. People can bring out the good side of you but be prepared because they can also be the reason why you can be a monster to some. So learned to say no and protect yourself,

People are really different individual, and you need to learn to accept who they are with their positive and negative attitude character. Do not ask them to change just because of community standard because once they will realize they are wrong it will be natural for them to change for a better version of themself. They have their own set of character that God allow them to be because God has a plan for every people in the world. And He give us the freedom to make a choice. And He is the only one that can judge us. I am thankful for those people who has been a part of my life and taught me a lesson, for those who are still part of my life and for those who will be part of my life. These people play a big role in my life they are the reason why I change a lot, it might be for good and for bad I am still thankful because of them I developed and realized a lot in life. And these people contribute to make me improve my thinking and to be better version of myself.

Friend

A friend is an individual that is somehow close to you and become part of your life. They are the people that are willing to stay by your side in spite or despite of your attitude. A friend is willing to listen to your opinion and will accept you for what you are. But what if you been betrayed by your friend, I can't imagine the pain and heart aches it will cause you. Because friendship is built by trust and once trust is no longer there it is hard to bring back the old connection.

I made my own definition of a friend, and this is F for Frank, they will be honest and direct to the point if there are something that they want to say because you deserve to know the truth. They will tell you a positive or negative information it will be your accountability how would you respond to it. Then R for Resembles, since you stay longer you are about to get a remembrance personality of that person, some traits and character can be adapted. And you will be having a thing that you usually have the same interest or hobby. Third is I for Influence, they can influence you to be a good or bad individual. However it will be your sole responsibility if you will be influence to do bad things. Just remember to put a limitation to protect yourself and check the consequence of your action. Fourth is E for Empathy, they are a good listener and they can feel the situation that you are in. They will be able to provide you a good advice and sometimes cracked a joke to make thing better. Of course they cannot remove the pain that you are going thru but they are a big help for you to vent out the negative emotion that you felt. Fifth is N for Nurture, they will take care of the friendship that you both establish, they will give importance to the connection that you made. All the memories that you have will be treasured. Last is D for Differences, you might have difference point of view different take on an event but you are able to respect their opinion and how they take the situation. True friend will accept you for who are and will be able to accept your good side and also your short coming. I do not have a lot of friend, but as for me it is better to have a few but a real one, and personally I do not know if that is also their definition of friendship. But as for me that is how I define it. One thing I learn with friendship is that you still need to set boundaries and limitation to avoid being hurt. You need to protect yourself and be cautious on everything because sometimes friends is also your enemy. But I can guarantee you that you will be able to feel if the people are sincere with their friendship. Plus think of a brighter side they can teach you a lot from that pain and you will become much stronger than before. So always thank them for the pain that they cause you since it will make you a much stronger and braver person. And when you learn to forgive you will be able to have a peace of mind and a peaceful life.

Accept your friend for who they are and be wise to adopt an attitude or personality that will be beneficial for you. Be open with their opinion but of course you are still the one who will be able to control your emotions. And set boundaries so that you will not get hurt along the way. I thank all my friends in the past, present and future for being there for me before at present and in the future. You are one of the reason for my self-improvement and for a better version of myself.

Best Friend

All of us encounter to be a friend to someone, we also experience that our friend come and go for a reason. And we also have someone that we call our best friend. It is a pleasure to have at least one friend that you can call your best friend. You can share anything and everything under the sun without hesitation because that person will not judge you for who you are.

In this life, it is hard to find a real person that you can trust. And I am lucky to have a best friend that I can considered real and tested thru time. We may not see each other in person frequently but once we do we have a lot to share a lot of happy moment and great experience to share. There is a connection within you, and you are happy on the achievement and their current situation. You are there to support each other and on a negative situation she is willing to listen to you all throughout until your negative emotion burst out and it just a great feeling to release those negative emotion and as if everything is already fine though the problem is still there. And aside from God that you can share your secret and embarrassment in life you can also share it with your best friend. But of course like I always said that you still need to have boundaries and limit so that you will not get hurt along the way. But I am happy that our friendship is already been tested in time and I can say that I can say everything with her. Our friendship is already over a decade and I am blessed to have her all throughout the sadness, happiness, and craziness journey of my life.

Hoping that you can also make the same kind of friendship and may you find the best friend that you deserve. A friendship that is not a basis of money, situation, status in life, and wealth, but a best friend who will accept you for who you are. We might not see them in person all the time but you are sure that in your heart she have a big space in it. She is also one of the reason fo who I am today and my inspiration to become a better version of myself.

God

Have you ever felt a very stressful and tiring day? Have you ever felt alone and being left behind on a corner of your room? Have you ever felt you are unable to voice out what you feel at the moment? Have you ever felt you do not have a person to talk to? Have you ever been to a situation that you are unable to find a solution to your current problem? Have you ever felt walking in hell on your day to day living? And you often ask if God really exist and hear, see us, and why he is allowing thing to happen?

As for me, I still believe in God in spite of all the negative experience that I encounter in life. I still believe in God even I am unable to see Him, because even I am unable to see Him I always feel His presence specially during the difficult times of my life. I can see His works during the storm, especially when I worked overseas that I do not have someone who could help me, and the sad thing is that our fellow countrymen is also causing you pain and is not helping you out. He is the only one that I can lean on and help me throughout the process. Thank God I am safely back home. And that is how powerful He is able to protect me and able to find a way just to beck in my country. God is the only one who can listen and never let you down in case you are facing a lot of challenges in life. All my darkest secret, all my embarrassment moment all my painful experience all my happy moments were all shared with Him and are all kept confidential. He is the only one I trust 100 percent. I may be on a difficult situation that I choose and made but He is always there to redirect and guide me. I always feel His presence especially when I am on my lowest point of my life. I am not a perfect Christian and I am nothing without God. I am not pretending to be pure but I just let my true personality comes out naturally. From all the storm in my Life I am thankful that I know help me out, I sometimes have time for Him because of busy schedule trying to get back on my feet, but I can feel that He is always there waiting for me to make time to pray and talk to Him. And sometimes I feel that if there are lots of problem arises, that is a sign that He is teaching me to pray and give time to do self-evaluation. Or it as also a sign for me to have a new beginning and reset my plans and goals. I strongly recommend to build a deeper connection with God because that will be the source of strength during the difficult times. You can invest love and time with God and I can guarantee you though we are living in Hell you can still smile and say I am strong and brave enough to fight the battle called life. You can feel a change within yourself that you can look at the trials on a positive way. But of course since we are only human and once our limitation that we set is already maximized we tend to break and might act on a negative manner. But the good news is that in spite of all the mistake that we committed in life God is a forgiving God and He is always listen to your explanation. He is not like a people who will forgive but never forget your mistake. He will also guide us to the right path and love us unconditionally. He also accept us for who we are, accept out positive and negative side. And most of all you will feel Safe even if you are walking thru the shadow of death you will not be shaken.

I am not perfect, I am naughty, I am sinful, I have lots of flaws but those are not a hindrance for me to have a connection with God. Being optimistic in life is what I learned recently by experience a never ending difficulties. But God taught me that I may never bring back the time but I can always make a new beginning and start a new plan and goal. He also taught me to focus on my personal healing and personal growth and to become a better version of myself.

www.ingramcontent.com/pod-product-compliance
Lightning Source LLC
Chambersburg PA
CBHW021324160726
47994CB00004B/1598